E   Battistoni, Ilse
BAT
        I fight fires

DEMCO

I fight fires.

PowerPhonics™

I Fight Fires

Learning the Long I Sound

Ilse Battistoni

The Rosen Publishing Group's
PowerKids Press™
New York

Dec. '02

I ride in a fire truck.

I drive to the fire.

I find the fire.

9

I go in to fight the fire.

I use water to fight the fire.

13

I fight the fire for a long time.

The fire is out!

17

I help a child find her mom.

19

I like to fight fires.

21

Word List

child
drive
fight
find
fire
I
like
ride
time

Instructional Guide

Note to Instructors:
One of the essential skills that enable a young child to read is the ability to associate letter-sound symbols and blend these sounds to form words. Phonics instruction can teach children a system that will help them decode unfamiliar words and, in turn, enhance their word-recognition skills. We offer a phonics-based series of books that are easy to read and understand. Each book pairs words and pictures that reinforce specific phonetic sounds in a logical sequence. Topics are based on curriculum goals appropriate for early readers in the areas of science, social studies, and health.

Letter/Sound: long i – Provide the child with a response card with the word *I*. Pronounce the following words, having the child hold up their cards when they hear the sound of **long i**, as in *I*: *fish, fine, yellow, red, ride, blue, bike, beet, bell, mine, five, like, side, time, nose, sale, kite*. As the child responds, list the **long i** words. Have the child underline **long i** in each word.
- Have the child name additional **long i** words. Add them to the list, and have the child underline **long i** in each of them.

Phonics Activities: Read aloud the following sentences, having the child name the **long i** word in each of them: "I have a friend called Mike." "I found a dime on the sidewalk." "One windy day, I flew a kite." "I saw pine trees in the forest." "I took a big bite of the cookie." "I am feeling fine." "I think this lunch box is mine." As the child responds, list the **long i** words. Have the child underline **long i** in each word. Have them tell other ways in which the words are alike.
- Write the word *fight*. Have the child form new words by replacing the initial consonant **f** with **l, m, n, s,** and **t**. Have the child decode the new words and underline the parts that are alike. Present the words *high* and *sigh*. Have the child tell how these are the same as or different from the words that rhyme with *fight*.
- Write the word *find*. Have the child form new words by replacing the initial consonant **f** with **b, k, m,** and **w**. Have them decode the new words and use them in sentences. Work in a similar way with *child, wild, mild*.

Additional Resources:
- Flanagan, Alice K. *Ms. Murphy Fights Fires*. Danbury, CT: Children's Press, 1998.
- Ready, Dee. *Fire Fighters*. Danbury, CT: Children's Press, 1997.
- Royston, Angela. *Fire Fighters*. New York: DK Publishing, Inc., 1998.

Published in 2002 by The Rosen Publishing Group, Inc.
29 East 21st Street, New York, NY 10010

Book Design: Ron A. Churley

Photo Credits: Cover © Richard Pharaoh/International Stock; pp. 3, 5, 7, 21 by Kelly Hahn; p. 9 © Ron Frehm/International Stock; p. 11 © Michael Hart/FPG International; pp. 13, 17 © Michael Salas/Image Bank; p. 15 © Stephen Wilkes/Image Bank; p. 19 © Scott Barrow/International Stock.

Library of Congress Cataloging-in-Publication Data

Battistoni, Ilse.
  I fight fires : learning the long I sound / Ilse Battistoni.
    p. cm. — (Power phonics/phonics for the real world)
  ISBN 0-8239-5928-7 (lib. bdg. : alk. paper)
  ISBN 0-8239-8273-4 (pbk. : alk. paper)
  6-pack ISBN 0-8239-9241-1
  1. Fire extinction—Juvenile literature. 2. English
  language—Vowels—Juvenile literature. [1. Fire fighters.] I. Title.
  II. Series.
  TH9148 .B38 2001
  628.9'25—dc21
                                    2001000193

Manufactured in the United States of America